Manifesto
Of A
Shrew

ISBN: 9798372127296

First printing edition 2022

Tribute To The Author

In grade school, Khae came home crying
'cause she felt bad she didn't defend
someone from bullying. I told her "see
that feeling, you never want to feel that
again, so ALWAYS speak up".
She ain't shut the fuck up since.

Your biggest supporter,
MOM

Preface

IN THIS BOOK I WRITE MY THOUGHTS
IN THIS BOOK I WRITE MY QUERIES.
IN THIS BOOK I WRITE ABOUT EVERYTHING
THAT HAS OR WILL MAKE ME ANGRY.
IT COULD BE MEN, THE WORLD, EVEN YOU...
AFTERALL IT IS THE MANIFESTO OF A SHREW.

-khaejenn

Table Of Contents

Women's History Month

I see you standing outside the fishbowl,
I ain't Nemo bitch.
Seeing never feeling,
Observing, just to make noncommittal
sounds.
We're pretty to watch right? So very
entertaining how we run round the tank of
the world with no end in sight.
You come with your fish food promises and
sprinkle JUST enough to keep us
satisfied.
Can't feed me though I'm sick of the
lies.
Your feminism feels like you're tapping
on the glass laughing with no cognizance
of how those taps shake up our world…
I see you standing outside the fishbowl,
I ain't nemo bitch.

Dear Diane

For a time, I was babysat by a lady of the night.
She told me I had a light in me 'cause I saw the demons she let in her body but still spoke to her with respect.
She'd say "it will take you far because respect is owed to a dog."
My only exception to that rule is if the dog is a man.
She would let me ask questions between her clients looking everywhere but my eyes, she proclaimed I "saw too much" as well as "she was too ugly to stare at too long".
Not even fathoming the same light she saw in me I felt pouring from her. If I had the words then that I have now I would have begged Diane to know I see her as a survivor.
That's the most beautiful thing of all.

A Query

"Why would I ever be ashamed of where I'm at when I can envision where I'm finna be?"

Myth

Your best years are all the ones you are
breathing.
We're told as women "don't waste your
best years!"
Those years where we are YOUNG, firm,
juicy… easily consumed.
As young girls men whisper to us "don't
waste your best years! Of course unless
its with me" Oh what a waste that would
be.
Never reaching our potential believing we
have an expiration date.
Magazines, Blogs, Mothers, Fathers all
making sure we feel that clock ticking so
in post mortem they can stand over our
shell murmuring
"she wasted her best years."
I just wish I could have told you…
Your best years are all the ones you are
breathing.

Socreteshia

No thought is new, in that I find
comfort.
I feel relief people have died knowing
these thoughts and shall be born
pondering them again.

Fiance Fido

Will you bark bitch?
It is no coincidence that man's best
friend is a being that can't talk.
One he controls, forever at his beck and
call.
A dog sitting at his feet waiting for a
scrap of attention.
A bone of affection.
Doing pretty tricks for his friends to
show how well behaved they are.
Begging for his approval.
Will you bark bitch?

A Query

"After picking my brain and eating my dreams, are you full?"

Mt. Viagra

I know why you're scared of falling.
It's always men that question me about
Peaking.
I know why you're obsessed with running
out of time
I know why you always have to be "on top"
'Cause only men have something on their
body that rises high to the sky hard and
strong then one day never peaks again.
I know why you're scared of falling.

Rick Murray

He's a nice guy huh?
Baby you gotta watch those nice guys.
They'll have you second guessing that
voice in your head, its not a gracious
voice but it's REAL.
That feeling in your stomach telling you
to look past the façade, those "something
not right" chills down your back.
You lucky huh?
Everybody saying "You got one of the good
ones."
Of course a devil in a suit looks better
walking you to hell.
What more could you want?
He puts you on a Pedestal that only he
can knock you down from.
Hes the only on that can catch you too…
him and no one else.
You look up from how far you've fallen to
find that you're all alone.
Hes a nice guy huh?
Baby you gotta watch those nice guys.

10

"Empathy has made an empty me."

Father Time

Time could only be a man.
Only they could be so cruel to slip from
your hands as you scream to hold them
close.
When I realized Time didn't belong to
anyone
Least of all me,
we got along so much better.

Hannibal

Of course the world tells you not to be bitter. That makes it so much easier to devour you.

Virgin No Suicide

Dear Wallflower, I love to see you grow.
Whether you become the brightest rose or
the strongest vine, just promise you'll
stay you.
STAY TRUE.
I know you tryna fade in the background
hoping the gardeners don't see how ripe
you're becoming.
Praying you don't get plucked.
'Cause who wants a wilted rose? Or a weak
vine?
You think it's safer I know, I just had
to tell you…
Dear Wallflower, I love to see you grow.

A Query

"How the fuck can your feminism be
radical, if what is radical to you is
life for us?"

Soul On Ice

When I say all men there is no "but"
I get it, how could someone's monster be
your hero?
Just as easy as Clark Kent can be
Superman.
One doesn't cancel the other.
I've never worn rose colored glasses when
it comes to the nature of male creatures.
Even if we share blood I can only see the
liquid as tears they've cause others to
shed.
I recognize the secret language.
The arm nudges.
Boys will be boys even at the expense of
girls…
Your father,
Your brother,
Your boyfriend,
Your cousin,
Your best friend,
Your husband,
YOU…
When I say all me there is no "but".

Mt. Life

Some humans see life as a hill or
mountain,
you peak then fall.
My life to me is a stream.
Sometimes fast.
Sometimes slow.
Every so often I'm blocked,
nevertheless, always flowing.
For there are some mountains you cannot
climb,
as well some hills you will die on.

A Query

"The meek shall inherit the earth,
what is here to inherit after "the
strong"?"

Casper

I distinctly remember discovering my
shadow as a child.
I realized it followed me everywhere,
whether I needed it or not.
Becoming an adult I distinctly remember
shame sneaking up on me in the same
manner.
Following me around,
A specter.
A cloud.
Raining on every thought, every
accomplishment.
Covering every inch of my skin.
Whether I needed it or not.

Mahsa Amini

Your Resilience is Resistance
I see you.
You can't say what your eyes scream.
You've been beaten into subjugation with
words and fists,
alas I see your clenched palm with
tearstained pillows.
You're a Sistah in arms though you can't
march with us.
You watch… with a heavy heart filled with
"what ifs"
You get up every day with your best foot
forward,
While someone else's boot is on your
neck.
I need you to know,
Your perseverance is power…
Your Resilience is resistance.

A Query

"Why would I worry about being jaded?
It's the most beautiful stone of all."

Vinegar Trophy

Often times women believe we'll be
rewarded for being nice.
I beg you...drown that hope in the same
honey you've been instructed to catch
flies with.

A Query

"Why do we treat the things we call
mother the worst?
Mother Earth
Mother Africa
Ma
Is it punishment?
Is that how we rationalize our abuse?
She birthed us when we never asked so she
deserves it?
How could we?"

OM

I won't wait until death for
reincarnation!
I'm birthing myself again.
This time I'll hug her a little tighter
before sending her on her way.
The next me may be the best me… or the
worst.
I'm still undecided.

Made in the USA
Columbia, SC
30 January 2025

52982463R00030